Beautiful
Southern
California

Beautiful
Southern
California

Text by Lee Foster

First Printing September, 1978
Published by Beautiful America Publishing Company
4720 S.W. Washington, Beaverton, Oregon 97005
Robert D. Shangle, Publisher

Library of Congress Cataloging in Publication Data
Foster, Lee 1943-
Beautiful Southern California
   1. California, Southern—Description and travel. I. Title.
F867.F68   917.94'9'045   78-8532
ISBN 0-915796-38-4
ISBN 0-915796-37-6 pbk.

Photo Credits

MARGARET ANNALA—*page 33, below; page 61, above.*

ROY BISHOP—*page 11, below; page 19, below; page 22, above; page 25, above; page 36, below; page 69.*

ROBERT CLEMENZ—*page 12 & 13; page 15, below; page 20 & 21; page 24; pages 64 & 65.*

ED COOPER—*page 9; page 18, page 23; page 32, page 51, below.*

JOHN GRONERT——*Page 16 & 17; page 25, below; page 40, above; Page 40, below; page 48 & 49; page 52 & 53.*

JOHN HOPKINS—*Page 43, below; page 46, below; page 55.*

ROY MURPHY—*page 10; page 33, above; page 37; page 41; page 44 & 45; page 47; page 50; page 56.*

ROBERT SHANGLE—*page 11, above; page 15, above; page 22, above; page 28 & 29; page 36, above; page 46, above; page 54, above; page 57, above; page 61, above; page 68, above; page 72.*

SAM AND BRUCE WHITE: *page 14; page 19; above; page 42; page 43, above; page 51, above; page 54, below; page 57, below; page 60.*

Beautiful America Publishing Company

The nation's foremost publisher of quality color photography

CURRENT BOOKS	FORTHCOMING BOOKS IN 1979	1979 CALENDARS
Utah	Massachusetts	Texas
Ohio	North Idaho	Hawaii
Texas	Pennsylvania	Illinois
Detroit	New Mexico	Florida
Alaska	Mississippi	Oregon
Georgia	New York	Colorado
Hawaii	Wisconsin	California
Arizona	Kentucky	Michigan
Portland	Maryland	Washington
Montana	Vermont	Western America
San Francisco	Virginia	
British Columbia	Illinois	
Oregon, Volume II	Idaho	
Southern California		
Western Impressions		
California, Volume II		
No. California, Volume II		
Washington, Volume II		
Lewis & Clark Country		

Send for complete catalog, 50 ᶜ

Beautiful America Publishing Company
4720 S.W. Washington
Beaverton, Oregon 97005

Contents

Enlarged Prints

of most of the photography
in this book
are available.
Send self-addressed,
stamped envelope
for information.
Beautiful America Publishing Company
4720 S.W. Washington
Beaverton, Oregon 97005

Introduction

The outgoing, optimistic, can-do attitude of Americans that foreigners find so refreshing receives its fullest expression in Southern California. Warmed by a benevolent climate, millions of migrants started a new life here. Other newcomers found the energy for a second start in life, while many journeyed here to savor their twilight years. Southern California exudes an optimism, a pleasure in newness. Characteristically, the new art forms of the 20th century, film and television, began here and find their primary sustenance here.

Southern California delights in superlatives, natural and man-made. Here you can find the oldest living things, the 4,500-year-old bristlecone pines, high in the White Mountains. The most massive living entity, the General Sherman Tree, a *Sequoia gigantea,* stands in a grove at Sequoia National Park. There is Mt. Whitney, at 14,496 feet the highest point in the contiguous United States, and Badwater, the lowest point. Among the lesser marvels are the Palisades Glacier, the southernmost glacier in North America; and Tulinyon Lake, the highest and deepest lake on the continent.

The natural extravaganza that is Southern California is rivaled by human accomplishment, especially in agriculture. Where else can you see oranges dangling from trees with a snow-capped mountain in the background? This is the paradoxical picture on Highway I-10 west of Redlands. The agricultural bounty of Southern California's dry Central Valley is a tribute to man's ingenuity as an importer of water. California produces 25 per cent of all the food eaten in the United States, including 40 per cent of the fresh fruits and vegetables. Holtville calls itself the Carrot Capital of the World; Indio, the Date Capital. But the superlatives only begin with agriculture. San Diego's zoo has the world's largest collection of wild animals. San Bernardino County is the largest county in the United States. Etc., etc.

Southern California will not appeal to the person whose style is understatement. Southern Californians live in the superlative mode, fearless of possible psychic inflation. Whoever can admire a brawny, lusty, sprawling, vital, and growing culture will find Southern California endlessly fascinating.

L.F.

The Deserts

For two days my family and I waited in our camper at the Panamint Valley on the west edge of Death Valley for the desert winds to subside. Visibility in the blowing sand was even less than in the heavy fogs or snowstorms familiar to me. Even with all the windows closed, the wind managed to sneak in and create a constant draft. Though our vehicle was nearly airtight, when we awoke in the morning there were small ridges of fine dust everywhere. Even my cameras within their plastic bags could not escape the windblown sands.

At the end of the second day, during a lull in the sandstorm, we watched a parade of cars and campers wind their way towards us from Death Valley. They moved slowly, as if wounded. When they stopped at the little grocery store oasis where we were parked, I looked at the vehicles, shaking my head in disbelief. Some of the vehicles had been stripped clean of paint by the blowing sand. All the cars had windows so badly pitted by the abrasive powder that they would have to be replaced. We retreated to a location other than the desert for the remainder of our vacation.

The desert, impenetrable on this occasion, graciously welcomed us on our next visit, in the spring. In Death Valley's Salt Creek we saw one of the most remarkable adaptations of life in the California deserts: the pupfish, *Cyprinodon salinus*. Five species of the small fish thrive in Death Valley and in the more northerly Owens Valley, living in isolated springs that may go nearly dry in summer and freeze almost solid in winter. Yet the small fish survive, even in the highly saline water. They are the remnants of great fish populations that lived here at the end of the glacial age, some 20,000 years ago, when the deserts of California were large lakes. In time, the lakes became verdant meadows, finally evolving to their present form.

Death Valley remains the California desert region of greatest interest to travelers, partly because of its splendor as a geological textbook. The proximity of the lowest and highest points in the 48 contiguous states, Badwater and Mt. Whitney, excites those who long for superlatives. Some visitors come to commune with themselves admist the sere elemental presence of Death Valley, as did the Desert Fathers of North Africa in the early Christian era. The saga of white man's first passage through the region, the 1849 expedition of William Manly, is a heroic tale of perserverance despite extreme deprivation. Borax and metal mining formerly lured the adventurous, but today the half-million annual visitors search for the blossoms of the California poppy as their reward.

Travelers who insist on fitting Death Valley into their summer vacation schedule will quickly learn the devastating accuracy of the place names, such as Furnace Creek. Piute Indians called the valley Tomesha, meaning ''ground afire.'' In spite of the forbidding demeanor of Death Valley a surprising range of plant life, more than 600 species, thrives here, including 21 species that exist nowhere else. The many kinds of small reptiles, rodents, and birds that live in the desert have the good sense to avoid the hot sun, and so are seldom seen by travelers. But their tracks on the dunes after a night's activity betray their presence.

Other desert regions of Southern California have their unique attractions. The most intense wildflower displays of my experience have occured in the Mojave Desert at Fairmont Butte near Lancaster, an area where a space shuttle may one day be built. Each spring admirers of these flowers put on a lavish show in Lancaster. Near Lancaster is Antelope Valley, one of the few remaining undisturbed areas of California. Here you can see fields of golden poppies, *Eschscholzia californica,* the state flower, stretching to the horizon. Lancaster is often called the Wildflower Capital of California. Blue lupines, goldfields, and many other species can be seen tucked among the poppies.

The Mojave Desert has an outstanding park, the Joshua Tree National Monument. The Joshua tree, a large lily plant with extended branches, reminded early Mormon settlers of the outstretched arms of the biblical Joshua. The Mojave desert covers nearly a third of the land area of Southern California.

The vitality of the desert becomes apparent only if you know how to look for it. An excellent available guide is the Living Desert Museum in Palm Desert, near Palm Springs. Separate gardens there reproduce and label plants from the low Colorado Desert and the high Mojave Desert. The James Irvine garden features the Joshua tree, plus 18 other succulents from the Mojave area. An interesting ethnobotanical garden features the plants that enabled Indians to survive by providing them food and fiber.

The high desert oasis in Morongo Valley, north of Palm Springs, is another accessible introduction to desert diversity. Bring your binoculars here to see some of the 230 species of birds, such as the brilliant little Vermillion flycatcher, that have been identified in the 80-acre Nature Conservancy and adjacent 160-acre Big Morongo Wildlife Reserve. The plant community here is a rich mixture of desert, coastal slope, and streamside species. Turn off to this unmarked gem at East Drive.

Palm Springs, nestled against the foothills of Mount San Jacinto, is an elegant retreat offering as its attractions a dependable sun and relaxation rather than a Disneyland or a Marineworld. In an effort to save the town from garish display, the city fathers decreed that no signs can blink or move and that no building can rise above 60 feet. The original idea for Palm Springs came from the mineral springs at the Spa Hotel, which still thrives. But today's visitor will probably be found at one of the 34 golf courses, 300 tennis courts, or 5,000 swimming pools. An aerial tramway can take you up 6,000 feet in 14 minutes, past five climatic zones, ending with a stunning view of the region. The Palm Springs Desert Museum includes an impressive diorama showing the surrounding Coachella Valley and Mount San Jacinto.

While other Indian tribes around the country are threatened with impoverish-

Continued on page 26

(Preceding full page) April's moisture brings greenery to the California deserts and snow to the summit of Mt. San Jacinto.

(Right) Water lilies grace a reflecting pond at Mission Santa Barbara.

(Left) Yucca and Golden Cup Oak grow on the banks of this stream on Pinyon Ridge, in the San Gabriel Mountains.

(Below) Setting sun lends a ghostly effect to the sand dunes in Death Valley.

(Following pages) Joshua Trees and other desert vegetation dominate the dry lands in Southern California's Joshua Tree National Monument.

(Opposite) In spring, wildflowers brighten the floor of Gold Valley, Death Valley National Monument.

(Right) Colorful fruit and fragrant blossoms in citrus groves are a Southern California hallmark.

(Below) Erosive forces carve wierd shapes from the soft sandstone of Red Rock Canyon, in the Mojave Desert.

(Following pages) Palm trees and a deserted archway are silhouetted against the blaze of a sunrise near Santa Barbara.

(Left) Wildflowers carpet a hillside near Gorman.

(Preceding page, above) Evening lengthens the shadows of the hills in Gold Valley.

(Preceding page, below) Winter's ice has not yet melted from Dollar Lake, at the foot of Mt. Clarence Kim in the Sierra Nevada.

(Preceding full page) Sunset provides bold lighting for a grove of orange trees and date palms.

(Left) Members of the lily family are among the flowers that flourish in Southern California where water is sufficient.

(Below) Snow melts late from the rocky slopes of Mt. Wheeler and The Needles, in the Sierra Nevada.

(Opposite) Clear waters give lie to the name of Dry Lake, in the San Gorgonia Mountain Wilderness Area.

(Following full page) Craggy peaks and tree-clad hills stretch out behind Moro Rock, in Sequoia National Park, the Sierra Nevada.

ment or displacement, the Agua Caliente band of the Cahuila Indians, who own much of the land in the Palm Springs area, are prosperous and secure. A few miles from the Canyon hotel they have set aside for visitors several striking and rugged palm canyons, delightful walks in the spring or autumn.

The severe desert environment is also more fragile than the grassland or forest ecosystems of Southern California. A five-inch-wide cactus in the desert may have spent the last century achieving its dimunitive splendor. Deserts were the last frontier for Californians, who have the urge to go everywhere. With the creation of ORVs (Off the Road Vehicles), especially balloon-tire Volkswagens and dirt bikes, much of the desert became accessible. California has more of these ORVs than any other state. The resulting devastation when masses of people came to the desert could easily be predicted.

The Bureau of Land Management, which oversees huge tracts of California desert, has banned the famous annual, 155-mile Barstow-to-Las Vegas motorbike race, which had been drawing 3,000 participants annually. Each year these races kicked up an estimated 600 tons of dust, more than a major dust storm. Many plants and animals along the route were destroyed by the swath of riders. The high-pitched whine of motorbikes there and elsewhere, breaking the desert solitude, was a separate issue. Government researchers have estimated that one motorcycle traveling straight for 20 miles alters severely and compacts the equivalent of one acre of land. A four-wheel drive vehicle causes the equivalent damage every six miles.

Much progress has been made on another issue, the preservation of Indian petroglyphs in the desert. The deserts and mountains of California have over 1,000 sites where ancient Indian petroglyphs can be found today. People who know of these sites generally try to keep them unpublicized because vandals and black market sellers, armed with high-speed drills and riding their ORVs, desecrate the sites. Some of the rock carvings go back as far as 3000-7000 B.C., a period archaeologists call the Pinto-Gypsum period. Barriers have been built at three major sites that enclose some 7,500 individual carvings. A determined corps of volunteers has gone to great lengths, sometimes camping out at the sites in shifts, to divert the energies of souvenir collectors and rifle shooters towards other targets.

(Preceding page, above) Winter's snows still cling to the rugged slopes of Mt. Williamson, highlighted by chilly late-afternoon sunshine.

(Preceding page, below) Native Southern California vegetation makes a colorful scene in Santa Barbara's Botanic Gardens.

The Great Valley

In 1875, a lady named Mrs. Tibbets plucked the first ripe orange in Southern California. The tree had been brought to her Riverside home from Brazil. More than nine million trees have descended from that first plant, which still bears fruit in Riverside today.

Driving east on I-10 toward Redlands, you can see today the image that lured more people to Southern California than any other single idea. In the foreground are orange trees, bulging with fruit, in a rich farmland reclaimed from the desert with imported water. In the background stand majestic snow-capped mountains.

Imagine an Iowa farmer receiving such a postcard from Southern California as the winter blizzards howled outside. Turning the image over in his mind, he thought of the spring frosts that killed his crops and the unpredictable summer rains that could wash out his fields or leave his seeds to perish in drought. For millions of midwesterners the card didn't need a ''Wish you were here'' written on the back. They came in a steady pilgrimage to the promised land.

Making the desert bloom was the passionate concern of generations of Southern California promoters. Nature seldom assisted them with adequate rainfall in the Great Valley, as the Central Valley was sometimes called. Today the Great Valley is synonymous with the most bountiful agricultural production in the state because of its complete irrigation systems, but for the 49ers crossing to the gold fields the region was known as the ''badlands.'' The Great Valley encompasses an area stretching some 50 miles from the Sierras to the coast range of mountains, running north from Bakersfield over 250 miles. John Muir, the noted conservationist, once wrote that in the Great Valley ''you could walk 400 miles and crush a hundred wildflowers with every footstep.''

Before the 20th century little substantial agriculture was possible here beyond sown wheat that was dependent on the vagaries of the weather. Today the sprawling farmlands and the huge human population throughout Southern California obscure the fact that the region is fundamentally arid. Seventy per cent of California's water supply falls in the northern third of the state as rain and snow, but today two-thirds of the water use occurs in the southern half of the state. About 85 per cent of the water goes to agriculture.

Occasionally nature reasserts the land's fundamental desert character in spite of man's best efforts to store and transport the water. Drought in the 1920s and again in the mid-70s brought ruin to many farmers and threatened the very existence of

(Following pages) A moment of stillness descends as the sun sinks below the horizon at San Clemente.

city life in Southern California, based as it is on imported water. Groundwater by late 1977 had been pumped out at record rates. California's entire agricultural industry teetered on the brink of disaster because it was uncertain that there would be any water available for 1978 plantings. Then came the inundating rains of January 1978, which changed the picture dramatically.

The wonder of Southern California agriculture is that the growing season never stops. While Iowa farmlands rest under three feet of snow, California's winter asparagus, grapefruit, and strawberries are being shipped out of the Imperial Valley. Imperial County would be a desert today rather than the 900,000-acre "Winter Vegetable Garden of the U.S." if it hadn't been for Colorado River water, first brought to the area in 1901 by the All American canal, now 200 feet wide and 80 miles long. Visitors to the region can see alfalfa, cotton, flax, melons, vegetables and grapefruit. The Coachella Valley is the only place in the United States where dates are grown commercially. The annual Date Festival in Indio, the Date Capital of the western world, is a lively time to visit.

California leads the country in 31 different crops, including staples such as grapes, lettuce and tomatoes, plus more specialized crops, such as dates. Some of the crops grown in Southern California are unique to the new world. The avocado is one of these; others, such as cotton, are ancient; and a few are new horticultural creations, such as the nectatine, born in the 1940s. The mind can scarcely imagine the staggering abundance of this food production. Can one conceive of the 11 million tons of produce grown in California in a given year, representing the top 30 crops? How does the mind grasp the five billion dollars paid for this produce?

In addition to possessing the three resources of climate, soil and imported water, Southern California agriculture benefited from the diverse backgrounds of farmers who came to the region with their special knowledges. The Basques of Bakersfield share their style today at several fine restaurants in the city. Chinese farmers came to Hanford, which is now famous for its fine Chinese restaurants. One of the newest state parks in Southern California is Allensworth, on State Highway 43, in Tulare County. Allensworth celebrates the first black community in the west. Lieutenant Colonel Allen Allensworth founded the agricultural town in 1906 after retiring from the Army with the highest rank attainable at that time by a black man. The town prospered until 1940 when agriculture in the area depleted the ground water by over-pumping. Whenever a part of Southern California is cut off from water, its lifeblood is gone.

The Great Valley has always been an important resting place for migrating waterfowl of the Pacific flyway. Teal, heron, snow geese, whistling swans, ibises, and sandhill cranes can be seen at the refuges north of Los Banos on the flood plain of the San Joaquin River.

Los Angeles Downtown

A small camera mounted over the escalator noted my presence as I descended to the underground of the ARCO (Atlantic Richfield) Towers, down to a world below the 52 stories of smoky glass at 6th and Flower. The presence of man was everywhere apparent, obscuring the few examples of potted and clipped nature. Even the metalwork sculpture that adorned the plaza from which I descended, Herbert Bayer's abstract stairs, "Double Ascension," mirrored an image of man.

Security dictated that my image and that of thousands of my fellows be caught on video tape that afternoon as we passed. Ironically enough, the area below ground was free of the smog above ground. The totally controlled and air-conditioned environment in the three levels of shops and restaurants—even a chapel—kept everyone comfortable. Acres and acres below ground formed a city within a city, with streets named after the famous avenues of the world, such as Bond Street, Via Veneto, and Place de la Concorde. Even the names of the streets were fitting for Los Angeles, which has a confidence that it can duplicate anything and perhaps even improve on the original.

My journey into the ARCO Towers epitomized Los Angeles, the most concentrated presence of man in Southern California. The towers and other surrounding skyscrapers signal a renaissance for the city. Los Angeles has long been famous as the ultimate example of urban sprawl, a condition caused in part by the use of materials and skills unequal to earthquake stresses. But recent progress in these areas has begun to change the face of the city. The new corporate downtown has given Los Angeles a visual center, plus a psychological hub that had been missing. Hoary jokes from the 1950s about Los Angeles being "seven suburbs in search of a city" have been retired. Today the center of the 450-square-mile metropolitan area is more than a cartographer's fantasy.

I returned to ground level and explored further the handsome iron and concrete urban forests that include the 62-story United Bank Building, tallest structure west of Chicago, the 55-story Security Pacific Building, and the 42-story Crocker Bank Building. As effective urban design, this core of buildings is one of the freshest architectural creations in the United States. My favorite example of high-rise aesthetics is the Security Pacific Building because its two tiers of gardens provide the intimate scale of a small park as well as a striking view of the area.

A stroll through the buildings leads an observer to the conclusion that the large corporations are today's major buyers of public art, especially sculpture. Alexander

(Preceding page) Springtime brings out dozens of types of wildflowers in the Antelope Butte Reserve, Antelope Valley, Los Angeles County.

Calder's "Four Arches" climbs 45 feet at the entrance to the Security Pacific Building. Frank Stella's bright acrylic paintings glow on the wall at Security Pacific. At the Union Bank plaza stands Alan Kirk's "Aquarius."

The renaissance of downtown Los Angeles can be dated from 1964 when the Music Center, a cluster of cultural buildings adjacent to the commercial skyscraper area, opened with violinist Jascha Heifetz playing Beethoven's Concerto in D Minor to the approval of wealthy donors.

The cornerstone building in the Music Center, focused around First and Grand, is the sedate Dorothy Chandler Pavilion, used annually for the Academy Awards and for many musical events, including performances by the Los Angeles Philharmonic. Adjacent is the moat-encircled Mark Taper Forum, which frequently hosts experimental theater. The Ahmanson Theater provides a setting for more traditional theater and musicals.

Nearby is the 32-story City Hall, for many years the tallest building in Southern California, standing above the 12-story limit that had been imposed because of earthquake dangers. From the observation deck at City Hall, on a clear day, you can see much of interest in the city.

The new downtown of corporate headquarters and the Music Center rises alongside, but does not obliterate, the older Los Angeles, especially the 40-acre historic center of the city, the Pueblo de Los Angeles State Historic Monument. The pueblo was founded in 1781 by 11 families from the Sonora and Sinaloa states of Mexico, which was then New Spain. At the direction of Governor Felipe de Neve, they marked off lots and began a town of 44 souls.

The area around the historic plaza, complete with its lyrical bandstand, has much of interest to see, especially the vitality of Olvera Street, a busy Mexican-style bazaar of outdoor shops, restaurants, and craft displays. The historical buildings ringing the plaza include the Merced Theater, the city's first; the Pico House, premier hotel of its time; the old Firehouse; and a chapel dating from 1784. Only a short walk west stands the Fort Moore Pioneer Memorial, a long bas-relief honoring the heroic men and women who settled Southern California.

Los Angeles' history includes a pastoral, bucolic 19th century before the rushing development of the 20th. The sleepy pueblo developed slowly when the Gold Rush contributed to the rapid growth of San Francisco. Two factors limited the Los Angeles population: insufficient water and a weak rationale for going there until adequate rail transportation provided opportunities for emigration and the export of produce. After California's isolation from the rest of the country ended with the first transcontinental rail line, in 1869, the rails gradually spread from Sacramento to Los

(Preceding page, above) Wildflowers and a lonely lighthouse brighten the headlands of the Channel Islands National Monument.

(Preceding page, below) The Chocolate Mountains are reflected in the still waters of an irrigation canal.

Angeles. The city fathers arranged for an adequate water supply partly by tapping the Owens River and running a pipeline 238 miles to the San Fernando Valley. Greater Los Angeles' gain was Owens Valley's loss, and bad feelings on this water issue run strong even today.

Another downtown monument, from a later era, is the Union Passenger Terminal, at 800 N. Alameda St. This railroad terminal, completed in 1939, is the last of the palatial structures created for the era when rail passenger transportation was the most attractive mode of travel. Rivaling in splendor even Omaha's marbled terminal, the cathedral to the rail era, this building consists of elaborate garden patios and a multicolored, domed interior, with red tile roofs and arches that echo the mission style of architecture. Today Amtrak signs in the lobby signal the possibility of a new age in rail transport.

Two other old favorites are still present in downtown Los Angeles. One of these is the 1893 Bradbury Building, at 304 Broadway. This early example is a lacy cast-iron filigree concoction whose grandly ornate interior has provided the backdrop for numerous television and movie films. Declared a city monument, it has been fully restored and is now used to house interior designers and architects.

Then there is the Grand Central Market, Broadway between Third and Fourth, still a cornucopia of sights, sounds and smells. Here you can buy almost anything edible produced on the earth and be entertained during the purchase with a babel of languages reflecting many exotic backgrounds.

The new and old downtown Los Angeles is one of the few places in the city where viable public transportation is available. For 10 cents an orange-and-white striped Mini Bus takes you from the corporate skyscrapers to the new Music Center, then to Old Town, and finally back to the area of Grand Central Market.

The lusty, sprawling, hungry vitality of the Los Angeles downtown suggests qualities that have made Los Angeles a difficult place to govern. As Southern California developer William Mulholland put it, ''I would rather give birth to a porcupine backwards than be mayor of Los Angeles.''

(Following page, above) A variety of brightly-colored plants and flowers may be found along the California coast.

(Following page, below) Rugged Mt. Langley, Lone Pine Peak and Mt. Whitney are visible in this Alhambra Hills view.

Greater Los Angeles— Orange County

Some descriptives regarding the Greater Los Angeles-Orange County region are "crazy-quilt," "maze of freeways," jigsaw puzzle." The variety is astonishing, from oil wells at Signal Hill in Long Beach to movie studios in Universal City. It's all somewhat like a bazaar—offering a way of life for every taste, plus a vast anonymity, a brilliant and almost uninterrupted sunshine, and ethnic diversity. The openness and freedom that Angelenos enjoy are definite aspects of their city.

Greater Los Angeles developed differently from other American cities, with their concentric patterns structured around a central core. Los Angeles includes more than 100 communities that are their own focal point, such as Hollywood. As Los Angeles spread out it incorporated these communities, or, if they chose to remain independent, simply continued past them, often enclosing them on four sides.

Promoters of Greater Los Angeles have never been accused of understatement. Today, when the face of the region is so urbanized, it is remarkable to look back at the words of an early booster, B. F. Taylor, whose *Beyond The Gates* reported in the 1870s, "Whoever asks where Los Angeles is, to him I shall say: across a desert without wearying, beyond a mountain without climbing . . . where flowers catch fire with beauty . . . where the pomegranate wears calyx crowns; where the bananas of Honolulu are blossoming; where the chestnuts of Italy are dropping; where the almond trees are shining . . . in the midst of a garden of 36 square miles—there is Los Angeles."

To the midwesterner reading these words while the blizzards roared outside, the dream of moving to Southern California became a consuming passion. In 1884 the Southern Pacific Railroad could carry the midwesterner away from the fury of winter for a $125 one-way fare. The next year the Santa Fe Railroad was completed and a rate war started. The fare dropped to only $5, and briefly even to the all-time low of $1 for passage to the promised land.

Greater Los Angeles-Orange County contains the largest human population in California and in the west—more than seven million people. Many growth industries, both manufacturing and high technology, have located in the benign climate. If solar

(Preceding page) Colored foliage highlights this meadow in the San Gorgonia Wilderness, San Bernardino Mountains.

energy becomes an important energy source in the future, Greater Los Angeles will be well situated.

The pleasures of the region are numerous for visitors with a purpose. Many persons like to see how a movie is made. The opportunity for this experience exists at Universal City and Burbank, where Universal Studios, Warners Brothers-Seven Arts, Columbia Pictures, Walt Disney Productions and the western flagship of the NBC television system are located.

Speaking of movies, climate was, once again, the reason why the film makers came here. The Southern California weather allowed a vast number of backdrops that early producers could use for scenic locales. With 300 sunny days a year, production schedules were seldom hampered by unpredictable weather. During a normal year in Greater Los Angeles only 38 of the 365 days of the year have a measurable 1/100th of an inch rainfall. D. W. Griffith shot feature films here before World War I. Cecil B. DeMille, Samuel Goldwyn, and Jesse Lasky, Sr. are credited with making the first feature-length picture in Hollywood, *The Squaw Man,* filmed in 1913-1914.

The most attractive respite from concrete in Greater Los Angeles is 4,200-acre Griffith Park, a gigantic green space as large as Beverly Hills. This municipal park was donated to the city 80 years ago by Colonel Griffith J. Griffith, who left a 3,000-acre land trust and funds to develop it. The hilly topography of the park at the base of the Santa Monica mountains discouraged the predatory pressures of developers in the era before the bulldozer. Today a panoramic view of the Greater Los Angeles region is possible from the Griffith Observatory day or night, smog willing. The terrain is mainly oak woodland and chaparal vegetation. Fifty-three miles of hiking trails acquaint the urbanite with a wealth of birdlife, small animals, and unobtrusive wildflowers. Many picnic sites are available.

The La Brea tar pits are a spectacle that no amusement park can match. In great pools of tar along 5800 Wilshire Boulevard many Ice Age mammals, such as elephants, camels, and horses, some now extinct, have been found. The animals fell into the tar while drinking water in the pools. Their bones were in many cases splendidly preserved so that their physical forms can now be recreated and interpreted. Recently the Page Museum was constructed at the site. There you can see the reconstructed skeleton of a giant Imperial Mammoth, largest of the animals trapped in the tar. After a walk from the museum to a viewing platform over the pits, you can look through a window at the paleontologists in their laboratory patiently cleaning new fossil bones recently dug out. The La Brea tar pits are commonly considered the largest and most important deposit of Ice Age fossils in the world, especially noted for extinct animals from the eras 14,000-10,000 years ago.

(Following page, above) The forbidding Anza-Borrego Desert is clothed in brilliant colors following spring rains.

(Following page, below) Fog settles on the lower mountains as dusk approaches in Sequoia National Park.

(Preceding full page) Abundant water makes possible the surprising lushness of 49 Palms Oasis, in the Joshua Tree National Monument.

(Opposite) Giant sequoias reach for the sky in this grove in Kings canyon National Park.

(Right) A Beavertail Cactus shows its brilliant blossom in Johnson Canyon, Death Valley National Monument.

(Below) The Trona Pinnacles are thought to have been formed by algae growing around hot springs on the floor of the lake that once covered the Mojave Desert.

(Following pages) Deep stillness typifies Jenke's Lake, in the San Bernardino Mountains.

(Left) This brilliant wildflower carries the descriptive name Red Hot Poker.

(Below) Desert Sand Verbena, Desert Sunflower and Dune Primrose cover the sands of the Yuha Basin. Signal Mountain, in Baja California, is in background.

(Opposite) A Clark's Nutcracker perches atop this snow-whitened fir tree on Baldy Saddle.

(Following pages) The rising sun reveals a placid sea at Summerland, south of Santa Barbara.

(Left) Desert springtime brings blossoms to the strangely-shaped ocotillo plant.

(Previous page, above) Ten Mile Creek roars over its rocky path through Sequoia National Forest.

(Previous page, below) The blue of the Colorado River south of Topock is in striking contrast to the barrenness of the mountains.

(Previous full page) Pine trees predominate in the San Bernardino National Forest.

(Right) A statue of Father Junipero Serra and an Indian child stands in the gardens at Mission San Juan Capistrano.

(Below) Sequoias tower over the forest floor in Kings Canyon National Park.

(Opposite) The floor of Death Valley stretches out from Aguereberry Point in the Panamint Mountains.

(Following full page) Water and wind-eroded forms dominate the rock-strewn Joshua Tree National Monument.

Greater Los Angeles also boasts a unique folk art creation, Simon Rodia's towers in Watts, 1765 East 107th St.

"I had in mind to do something big, and I did," Simon Rodia said, after many years of work.

An Italian tile setter, he was 40 years old when he started weaving the weblike towers at his modest home in Watts, using whatever urban discards came to hand, including shells, broken dishes, red tail lights, and blue Milk of Magnesia bottles. Working with no design in mind, he piled up his towers eventually to 55, 97, and 99½ feet. For 33 years Rodia worked on his towers, but finally in 1954 he stopped, deeded his property to the city, and dropped from sight, turning up later, before his death in 1965, in an obscure northern California town.

Much litigation and debate ensued. Were the towers an art creation worth preserving? Citizen committees said yes and such prestigious organizations as New York's Museum of Modern Art lent support. Were the towers safe? Where would the funds come from to support them? Not until the 1970s were these questions settled affirmatively. In Los Angeles, the American fantasyland, it is fitting that Rodia's towers survived, a curious monument to the fantasy visions of one man.

Among the repositories of art and culture in greater Los Angeles, perhaps the most impressive is the 200-acre Huntington Library and Art Gallery in San Marino. There you can see a copy of Gutenberg's Bible, Ben Franklin's autobiography in his own handwriting, a First Folio of Shakespeare's plays, and George Washington's hand-written geneaology. The extensive gardens include elaborate desert, palm and herb plantings. The 10-acre cactus garden claims to be the world's largest collection of cactus and succulents.

Orange County is synonymous with the word "attractions." The three most prominent are Disneyland, Knott's Berry Farm, and Lion Country Safari. Disneyland remains the premier attraction in Southern California. Surprisingly enough, more adults than children each year visit the Magic Kingdom's Main Street, USA, Tomorrowland, Adventureland, Frontierland, and Fantasyland. It could be safely said that Disneyland has provided more happy escapist memories for more people than any other place in the country.

Knott's Berry Farm celebrates the Southern California agriculture and the enduring myth of the American West. Walter and Cordelia Knott arrived in a Model T Ford in 1920, rented a small farm, grew berries and sold them at a berry stand. In 1927 they expanded to sell hot biscuits and pies, in 1934, they added chicken dinners, and after World War II, steaks. Today their children and grandchildren

(Preceding page, above) Brilliant claret-cup cactus blooms in the shadow of a rock on the California desert.

(Preceding page, below) Panamint Daisies enliven the harsh desert landscape near Wildrose Canyon, Death Valley National Monument.

manage the enterprise, which includes ghost towns, vaudeville shows, an Indian village, gold panning exhibits, and staged train robberies.

Lion Country Safari near Newport Beach represents a new concept in zoos, caging the people in their cars and letting the animals run free. Animals from Cheetahs to white rhinos, ostriches to zebras, roam their individual savannahs, a striking approximation of the native African or Asian habitats.

The Mountains

The Sierra Nevada Range, a visual symphony, stretches for 400 miles along the eastern half of California, averaging 70 miles in width and reaching its highest point, 14,495 feet, on Mt. Whitney.

One of the treasures of Southern California plant life is the bristlecone pine tree high in the White and Inyo Mountains east from Bishop. The oldest living things on earth, these trees have been core-dated at 4,500 years. Fallen trees in the area have been dated at 9,000 years. These trees were already aged when Socrates flourished in fifth-century Athens. There is hardly a better example anywhere of the tenacity of nature, the will to survive. The trees may be seen at the Schulman Grove interpretive center at the Methusaleh Grove, near each other east of Big Pines. At Schulman is Pina Alpha, 4,300 years old. Methusaleh has a tree 4,600 years old.

The other arborial marvel of the Sierras is the *Sequoia gigantea,* which was once thought to be the oldest as well as the most massive living thing. The title of oldest was surrendered to the bristlecones, but the big trees are a sight to see, especially the General Sherman tree at Sequoia National Park. The trees are found from north of Yosemite south to the California Hot Springs. The ''Giant Forest'' grove in Sequoia National Park is the largest collection. General Sherman is 272 feet high, 101.6 feet around at the base, and 3,500 years old. A related tree, the coast redwood of northern California, grows taller but is less massive.

In the eastern high mountains the Owens Valley is a lovely drive, especially on Highway 395 from Big Pine to Lone Pine. Further north, in Mono County, lies Southern California's ski area, Mammoth Lakes. Trout fishing, deer hunting, and guest ranching attract people to the Owens Valley, noted for its clean air and the sparkle of its sunshine.

The high eastern valleys of the Sierras have many minor places of interest. In Laws, at the Laws Railroad Museum, are the old rail cars that served the Nevada mines. Fifteen miles north of Laws you can see Indian petroglyphs by taking U.S. 6 to

(Following page) A small, rushing stream brings a touch of green to Johnson Canyon, Death Valley National Monument.

the carvings along Fish Slough Road. A circle trip via Casa Diablo Road brings you back to U.S. 6. A creek wash with many petrified fragments lies west of Coaldale. By turning south on State 3 for 10 miles, then left at a signal, ''The Sump,'' for two more miles you arrive at the fossilized beds. Enthusiastic rock collectors can also scour the area for opals and Apache tears.

There are more than 2,000 mountain lakes and streams to fish in the southern Sierras. Bishop is the starting point for anglers who seek trout in Pine and Bishop creeks, Bishop Park, and many other waters up to 10,000-foot elevations. Each spring, fishermen bring their first day's catch in for prizes and comparison on Rainbow Trout Day.

From Big Pines a lateral road leads to a close look at Palisades Glacier, the southernmost glacier in the Northern Hemisphere. Another natural spectacle, the Devil's Postpile, consists of columns of hot lava that cooled to split into perfect vertical layers, 40 feet thick. Above Lone Pine you can see a cluster of high mountain peaks, the highest skyline in California, with Mt. Whitney only slightly higher than the others. The Mt. Whitney fish hatchery out of Big Pine is both a regal place to fish and the origin of many of the big ones that didn't get away.

Along the coast of Southern California stretch several ranges of coastal mountains that are lower than the Sierras. One of the interesting trips possible here is to the Mount Palomar Observatory east and north of San Diego. A trip to Palomar gives you not only wild back country mountain terrain but also several historical sites and museums that celebrate the Spanish, Indian, mission and astronomy cultures of the San Diego region.

In driving to Palomar the East Grade Road is recommended because it is a more gentle climb, especially for cars that overheat. Starting at Lake Henshaw, which offers catfish, bass, and crappie fishing, the drive up the side of the mountains opens up sweeping vistas to the west. In summer the phenomenon of the inversion layer traps the cool ocean air.

Within the Palomar Mountain Park (Palomar is Spanish for ''place of the pigeon''), rustic walks are possible in Doane Valley and at Cedar Grove. A self-guided nature walk through Doane Valley acquaints you with mountain flora. The area was once used by horse thieves to shelter their animals. George Doane arrived in 1880 and planted apple orchards, raised hay, and ran hogs.

An interesting back-country road, the Nate Harrison Grade, can take you down to the Pauma Valley for a trip through the mountain foothills to the sea. Rangers at Palomar Mountain Park can inform you if the road has been recently graded. Nate Harrison was a slave who came west with his master in 1848. He farmed here until he died, age 101, in 1920. A bronze marker in a stone shrine midway down the road

(Preceding page, above) A variety of spiny cactuses appear in the Living Desert Reserve, near Palm Springs.
(Preceding page, below) Sunset colors the sharply-etched reflection of trees in the Salton Sea.

recalls Harrison, naming a spring in his honor, and sums up his life with Robert Burns' refrain, "A man's a man for a' that." From the grade you can see the miracle of water in the desert, several large reservoirs, some surrounded by young avocado and orange groves.

From Palomar you can take a leisurely trip down the San Luis Rey River valley, following the foothills of the mountains as they descend to the sea. You might stop off for a visit to the "King of Missions," Mission San Luis Rey, and to its branch or "assistencia," San Antonio de Pala, a mission that still serves the coastal mountain Indians.

San Diego

From the hills of Point Loma above San Diego Bay I scanned with my binoculars the Pacific, the San Diego skyline, and the Naval shipyards on the Bay.

I wonder if the pleasure I took in looking down at the land and water from this vantage point, the most southerly site on the California coast, was as intense as the joy felt in 1542 by the Portuguese navigator, Juan Rodrigues Cabrillo, when, buffeted by storms that threatened his survival, he looked up at the high spur of land where I stood. Cabrillo's sighting was the first contact by a white man with California. Spain, the dominant sea power of the day, was pushing ever farther north from New Spain, as Mexico was then called, in search of precious metal and possible trade.

The explorer's imagination had been excited in part by the novels of one Garcia Ordonez de Montalvo, whose book, *Las Sergas de Esplandian,* in 1510, talked of an unusual island paradise, called Califa's land, California. Montalvo wrote, "know that, on the right hand of the Indies, there is an island called California, very near to the Terrestrial Paradise, which was peopled by black women . . . their arms were all of gold."

Antonio de Mendoza, the Mexican viceroy who funded Cabrillo's voyage of discovery, gave him explicit instructions "to examine the western side of California as far north as possible, seeking particularly for rich countries and for passages leading to the Atlantic." Cabrillo characterized San Diego Bay as "a very good closed port."

In the next two centuries the British explorers and later the Russian fur traders flirted with the California coast, causing some uneasiness for Spain. A new concern arose for Spain when Britain assumed control of Canada from the French. In 1769 Spain authorized three ships to leave the southern ports of Baja for San Diego Bay. Such were the terrible odds of the day that only two of the ships reached their destination, where the scurvy-ridden sailors limped ashore. An overland expedition to

(Left) The hardy Bristlecone Pine has been recognized as the earth's oldest living thing.

San Diego suffered similar privations, but by July 1 of that year all the survivors had arrived. The town and mission of San Diego began, with Gaspar Portola as the secular authority and Junipero Serra as the religious leader.

The hospitable port has continued to define the fortunes of San Diego down to the present day. Perhaps most noticeable to the visitor, gazing down from Point Loma, are the squadrons of naval ships in the Bay. A tour of history is the most fitting way to approach this most historical of Southern California cities. In one full day you can visit the six key historic San Diego area sites in this efficient order: the Cabrillo Monument, the *Star of India* ship at the Embarcadero, the Hotel del Coronado, Balboa Park, Old Town and Presidio Park, with its museum to Father Serra, and the Mission San Diego de Alcala.

Equipped with a good San Diego city map, you can begin at the Cabrillo Monument, at the tip of Point Loma, west of the central part of San Diego. The Cabrillo Monument is a fitting place to start both because of its historic primacy and its commanding view. The Point Loma promontory, as might be expected, was a treacherous, rocky place for ships, which prompted construction of the Point Loma lighthouse in 1855. Operational until 1891, when a lower lighthouse that was more effective in fog replaced it, the Point Loma lighthouse is now a museum describing how the keeper and his family amused themselves during long periods of isolation.

Circling north and east around San Diego Harbor brings you to the Embarcadero, mooring place for the oldest iron-hulled merchant ship still afloat, the *Star of India*. The ship is now a museum, particularly informative about workaday sea life in the 19th century, with its cramped bunk quarters and the sea biscuit kitchens, the shipwright's tools, and the surgeon's instruments. All these artifacts take you back to the days when voyages lasted for years and the ship was its own self-contained world.

South and across the bridge west to Coronado rises the famous Hotel del Coronado, a monument to late 19th century opulence. This resort complex is the largest wooden structure in the nation. In 1885 Elisha Babcock and H. L. Story bought the land and build Babcock's dream, a hotel "that would be the talk of the western world."

Back across the bridge and north is San Diego's famous Balboa Park, first set aside in 1868. There is a local saying, partly true, that San Diego was built around a park. Best known for its elaborate zoo of 5,000 animals, the world's largest, the park has a faintly Spanish-Moorish motif in its architecture, heritage of the 1915 Panama-California-Pacific International Exposition. The park is a fine picnic and walking area with several museums and some botanical surprises, such as a sprawling Australian tree, a Moreton Bay fig, which children might well vote the most climbable tree in the world.

The earliest settled part of San Diego, now called Old Town, lies southeast of the intersection of highways 8 and 5. This collection of dwellings dates from the Spanish,

Mexican, and early American period. The historic section is bounded by Wallace, Congress, Twiggs and Juan streets. Among notable buildings in Old Town is the Whaley House, oldest brick structure in Southern California.

In the adjoining Presidio Park, where a small garrison of soldiers once protected the first mission, is the Serra Museum, a monument to the intrepid Franciscan. Six miles farther east along Highway 8, on the left side of the road, stands the white facade of the oldest California mission, San Diego de Alcala, founded by Junipero Serra in 1769. On Mission Gorge Road is the site where Father Serra moved the original mission from Old Town so it would be closer to Indian settlements and a fresh water supply. The museum at the mission includes records in Serra's own hand.

San Diego is particularly pleasing to the traveler who wants to discover the roots of Western history.

The Coast

The sea otter swam playfully in front of me, not more than 10 feet offshore, rolling over on its back, holding a small abalone against its chest with one paw, clutching a rock with the other. By rapidly whacking the shell with the stone, the otter was able to crack the abalone and then chew out the succulent meat. After letting me witness his meal, the otter disappeared back into the kelp beds.

I was walking near the north end of the Southern California coast at Point Lobos Nature Reserve, Big Sur, a place where many of the pleasures of the coast can be experienced. The reserve took its name, lobos (''wolf''), from the barking of the California and Sellar sea lions that inhabit the offshore rocks. As a unique outdoor museum the reserve offers visitors a look at cormorants, pelicans, and coastal ducks, such as the Brandt. Here are fine examples of the twisted Monterey Cypress, the stalwart trees that brave the malforming effect of incessant winds. For the scuba diver there is a unique underwater park, 750 acres of undisturbed plant and animal life. Away from the shore deer walk in the meadows and lacy lichen clings to the tree branches. Wild lilacs perfume the hiking trail, red algae on the dead tree trunks exhibit colorful decay, and golden poppies sway in the meadows. Point Lobos is one of the best picnic spots along the coast at which to uncork the fine wine, open the sourdough bread, and break out the cheese.

Sighting the California grey whale during its annual migration is one of the spectacular encounters available along the Southern California coast from Point

(Following page, above) Point Lobos Lighthouse overlooks the sea at San Diego.
(Following page, below) These strange, erosional formations are on the north side of Mono Lake in the Sierra Nevada.

Lobos to Point Loma. Charter boats from San Diego can carry you close to the whales without disturbing these large mammals. From December-February you can see the 11,000 whales making their annual 6,000-mile journey from cool Arctic waters to their calving and breeding grounds at Scammons Lagoon and other sites in Baja. The existence of these large animals today is a conservation success story, because they once hovered on the edge of extinction. Protecting the whales has enabled them to regain a stable population level.

The grey whales reach a length of 35-45 feet and weigh up to 30 tons at maturity. Newborn calves are also large, 16 feet long and 1,000-1,500 lbs. Observers watching the whales from a charter boat may see them blow several times, then descend, but a competent boat operator, gauging their speed and direction, can put his boat to within a few yards of where they will rise again. Along the Southern California coast the whales travel close to shore, and can be seen easily with binoculars. Many surfers have had the surprise of their lives as the whales passed them by. The shortening days of sun in the Arctic, reducing the plankton yield, stimulate the whales to make their migration.

Driving south from Point Lobos, after passing the Santa Lucia chain of the coast mountains, the next major stop is William Randolph Hearst's ''castle,'' San Simeon. The extravagant residence, built by the publisher and heir to the Comstock Lode, is, to put it mildly, a spectacle worth seeing. Three large houses rest on a coastal knoll overlooking the sea. One hundred twenty-three acres of gardens, terraces, pools, and palatial guest houses create a setting for the giant 137-foot-high Hispano-Moorish mansion that Hearst called La Casa Grande. Today the grounds are a state park visited by close to a million people annually.

The next major stop, moving south along the coast, is the Santa Barbara area. The Indians of the Santa Barbara coast, the Canalions, were among the most advanced of the estimated 133,000 Indians in California in 1770. They were noted for their wooden canoes of lashed planks, a construction found nowhere else in North America. They were able to move in these boats with great skill and speed.

The coastal mountains in the Santa Barbara region are the last remaining habitat for the stately California condor, the largest bird in North America. With their numbers now diminished to less than 20 members, the condor hovers precariously on the abyss of extinction.

Santa Barbara is the Southern California city that has perpetuated the Spanish Mission style of architecture most pervasively. The design that started the trend in the area is the Santa Barbara Mission, one of the finest restored California missions. Later echoes of the style can be seen in the presidio or fort from the era when Santa Barbara was a military outpost for Spain. A visit to the mission, at 2201 Laguna, is well worth your time. The pleasing symmetrical towers and graceful design have

(Preceding page) Touches of snow still are evident in the shady forest near Baxter Pass in this springtime view.

helped make this the most photographed of the missions. Such amenities as a stone fountain of striking yet simple design do much to enhance the structure, dating from 1808. However, an adjacent graveyard with a purported 4,000 Indian bodies is a sobering reminder that smallpox, measles, and other European-introduced microbes doomed the Indian population of California, regardless of the good or ill will that the foreigners felt for them. The excellent condition of the mission arises from the fact that the buildings have remained continuously in the hands of the Franciscan Order. Since the 1850s the mission has served as a training ground for the Franciscans.

Already in the 1920s many Santa Barbara city fathers were pressing for a Mission Revival and Spanish Colonial style for the city. They received an unexpected assist at 6:40 a.m. on June 29, 1925, when an earthquake (6.5 Richter) destroyed the downtown area, allowing the planners to start afresh. Their handiwork is displayed along State Street and in the 72-square-block downtown area called El Pueblo Viejo. You can get a good detailed walking map at the Chamber of Commerce, 1301 Santa Barbara Street.

Along the Los Angeles-area coast—fully 105 miles of beaches—a stop at the Malibu-Surfrider State Beach, west of Malibu Pier, will acquaint you with the archetypal Southern California sport, surf riding. The sandy-haired youngsters come streaming in on their boards, carried by some of the best surfing waves in the world. Sometimes tournaments are in progress, making the event a spectator sport. The first surfer, George Douglas Freeth, performed twice a day in 1907 below the Victorian Hotel Redondo in Redondo Beach. A promoter of the hotel had found Freeth in Hawaii and persuaded him to come to Los Angeles. Freeth performed at noon and again at 4 p.m., convenient times for the packed tour buses that would bring hundreds of people out, as one reporter said, ''to see the man stand on the water.''

Long Beach is also the port where you can take a boat to Santa Catalina Island, largest of the offshore islands along the Southern California coast. Since 1887 the island has been a popular vacation spot. The small seaport of Avalon is the only development. Across the island's 21-mile length are trails for hiking or guided back-country tours. You can take the boat out for a few hours' visit or else arrange to stay overnight. Avalon's oval Casino was the broadcast point for many of the big bands of the 20s-30s era of radio. The famous glass bottom boat tours to the clear seas around Avalon should not be missed because of the extensive fish life lurking in the kelp beds. Some of the underwater area has been set aside as an underwater state park.

Whatever in Southern California appeals to you most, whether that be images from nature in the deserts, mountains and coast, or the works of man in such major cities as Los Angeles and San Diego, there is no disputing that for sheer diversity and vitality, the region has few peers.

(Following page) Mormon settlers, traversing the desert, named the Joshua Tree for the Biblical prophet Joshua. This one is in Joshua Tree National Monument.